5 Steps to Freedom;
from a life filled with pain!

S. Allen Mosley

Content

Content

Introduction

After writing "Finding the Joy in Cancer" and "Seasons of Change." I needed to tell more about my personal story. For years since my first cancer diagnosis, everyone has asked me to share more of my own story. When the third cancer diagnosis came along and brought a great deal of chronic pain, I knew it was time to finish what had long been on my to-do list.

Both of these books have been an Integral part of my life, and I utilize them daily in my spiritual practice. When you are going through cancer or any major life event, it helps when you can share it so that others can evolve and grow with you. I am always asked about my personal story, what was it like growing up in the rural south being a gay man and how do you feel about it now?

Often the things that we don't wish to talk about are the things that bring us the greatest deal of discomfort. Today I know I am deeply loved by my parents and family. It has been an arduous journey along each step of the way but well worth the process. Learning to love myself through the hidden beliefs was quite the journey, yet I would do it all again to find my Tony.

The premise of this book is about healing those hidden beliefs and how we grow through those and change those into new beliefs that allow us to evolve and become the people we are destined to be. Often we build a family in a multitude of Ways. Some we chose and some we are born into; both are equal importance.

As you step into your new life, I urge you to take this work one step at a time and with the utmost integrity and love for yourself, knowing that as you step forward in love, you are creating a life worthy of respect and honor. Often as we climb the steps and begin to change our lives, others will do their best to diminish the work that we are doing. We must not allow that to detour from our work in any way. Each step is a stride toward freedom from pain, freedom from the life we have lived for other people, freedom from a life in which we played small so that others could be happy. It is now time for us to live boldly as who we are.

I remember the introduction of my book, "Seasons of Change," that talks about the germination of the seed. For the seed to grow, it is planted, covered in soil, where it sits in complete darkness until it is cracked open from the inside. Knowing full well what its potential is, the seed opens from the inside and sends out that which is within itself through the soil up into the atmosphere. How often in our lives do we feel we live in darkness? How often do we feel like we are in despair or out of control or alone? In those moments, if we are willing to be vulnerable, we can open ourselves from the inside, and share our divine gift like the seed.

Each of us has a destiny for greatness, a consciousness with unlimited possibilities. What we do with that is up to us. We can die with it in us, or we can plant it, be vulnerable, open up, and allow that which is within us to flourish, grow, evolve, and share it with the world. Whatever you choose, know that you are deeply loved.

Dedication

To my husband Tony, you are my biggest supporter, loving companion on this journey we call life. I would walk one trillion steps to walk a step with you. You will forever be my greatest gift. I love you.

To my brother Keith, Thank you for your tireless work in making sense of my book, and for using your brilliance to edit it with love.

To my Daddy, Thank you for your never-ending love and the way you show up in my life as love today.

Step 1

I believe we call into our lives the people we need to help us grow, evolve, and enrich our lives. Everyone in our lives is a teacher. Some we choose, and others show up when it is time to move forward. Sometimes we go with ease; other times we go kicking and screaming, yet we move forward all the same. I have had some at the same time. To say that cancer has cracked me open from the inside out would be an over exaggeration of the word. However, it was that opening that allowed me to understand that I no longer wanted to live the way I had been living, and for a year, I took a different path. That path led me to self-discovery and self-love and the desire to change the way I loved myself and those around me. (The fact of the matter is that I understood I had not loved myself at all.) I had a sincere desire to have someone who would join me on that quest to change. I had discovered to love someone else, I had to first love and honor who I was. I had to embrace all of the past and the present and enfold that into what I intended for the future. There would be no more leaving bits and pieces of me here and there hoping that no one would discover them along the journey. Whoever was to love me had to love all of who I am as I did or nothing at all.

To say that I was ready for cancer or that I wanted it in my life when it arrived would be an exaggeration. It was a pain like I had never felt before, yet there was something within me that led me to the doctors and something within me that refused to be dismissed when they said the lump in my neck was nothing and it would go away in a few days.

There was a fear, a great fear, and yet I knew deep within that I was ready to embrace and embark on a journey of a lifetime. At that moment, I didn't understand boundaries, because, to be honest, as a white male I had never had to look at them or understand them. Everything I knew about boundaries had always been in regards to land, ownership, and possession. I was traveling into something new that was quite frightening. Yet my soul knew I was ready to receive.

What are the things that open us up to growth? Most of us never sign up for growth on a personal level in our lives unless we are fortunate enough to be able to afford college or some form of advanced training. Once that is complete, we may take a few extra credits here and there or a workshop, but few of us grow past the level of discomfort in our lives. This means that many of us stop doing the/our work in our lives once we start to feel any pain.

That is the number one reason why gym memberships are so easy to get into and so challenging to cancel. Most people continue to pay rather than put effort into getting out of the membership. In this example, we don't feel the pain of the monthly fees because they charge our account automatically, and, therefore, we don't feel the sting as if we would if we were mailing the check ourselves each month.

If we don't see it, we don't feel it. How many people balance their budget the way they did ten years ago? Everything has changed with online banking and automatic billing, and we trust it to all work correctly. The drawback is that we often forget about it.

Gym membership, video viewing, online gaming, and more. We spend millions of dollars each year on things we don't use. However, the pain is not significant enough for us to feel it to change. Therefore, we have EMBRACED these boundaries because we have become comfortable with them.

When I EMBRACE a boundary, it means that I

Emotionally
Move
Boundary
Radius
Around
Current
Experience

We can do this with blinders on like horses being led where they are told, or we can do it with the courage that we are now ready to take on the next level of growth in our lives. We can take back the power that has been ours all along. Either way, I assure you that you will EMBRACE life in one way or the other. The choice of how you do it is up to you.

How do I EMBRACE so that I can move forward?

Many of us don't understand how boundaries work in our lives, and we don't want to talk about it. Everyone needs healthy boundaries, and everyone needs personal space. Webster's defines "boundary" as, "something that indicates or fixes a limit or extent." We need to understand our limits or the extent at which we are willing to go in a relationship. Most importantly, the relationship with ourselves.

When we do not, we often find ourselves in a great deal of pain, and we hurt so deeply we don't understand why.

Example:
As someone who has limited walking ability, I understand my boundaries and the fact that I need assistance when walking. I walk at a slower pace, rest frequently, and I can't walk for long distances. As wonderful as a long walk on the beach might sound, I have to be mindful of my boundaries or I will soon find that I am out on the beach in a great deal of pain.

Pain is an excellent motivator. It is one of the most significant reasons why we move in any direction in life. Whether or not we learn in the process is entirely up to us! When we are children, we learn through pain - most often by experience: when we touched the stove, when we were stung by a wasp, or when someone hit us. At that moment, we took in the experience, cried, ran to our parents or guardians who comforted us and sent us on our way. Depending on the size of the hurt, we decided to continue the adventure or not to have that experience again. Pain teaches us quickly about life, and those we love do their best to keep us from experiencing anything that remotely feels like pain of any kind. We do our best to forget the experience altogether as if we are in a state of amnesia. We act as if it never happened, and should we experience it again, we find ourselves in this deja vu where we remember the pain from before. Somehow the healing is a natural process and part of a rhythm that seems quicker due to the memory of what happened before.

I like to call this: Universal Life, a life in which we are gaining knowledge through daily living. Each of us does this in our own way. Each of us came here with a set of intentions and lessons to learn, and we need certain teachers or events along the way to aide us in that growth process (Evolution). As those lessons appear, we often have resistant to this process, and as this happens, we push against life itself, which causes friction that most often causes growth, pain/suffering, and change in our lives.

Example:
We say, "I need more patience in life." The alarm clock doesn't go off and we are running late for work again. We run into a traffic jam on the way into work, and we notice the gas tank is on empty, and we have to stop and get some gas. We get off the road and find that our favorite gas station is closed for renovations and the closest one is four miles away in the wrong direction. And suddenly, we remember we asked for patience yesterday while we were at work, and the universe said, "YES!"

Many times, we become attached to where we are and do not want to let go of the people, places, or things that we have grown accustomed to. We also don't want to travel into the unknown, so we resist it, choosing instead to stay in our current situation knowing that it is incapable of bringing us happiness, joy, or pleasure. We will remain here for one simple reason: it is familiar! The torment of the known is far better than the chance of utopian in the unknown.

That is why I talk about pain being one of the best motivators. Most of us refuse to go to the doctor until the pain is so great that we have no other choice. We see no need to have an annual check-up because we feel fine. Some have a fear of doctors in general, but a lot of people in the United States have a history of abuse that is then passed down generationally. The history of the Tuskegee experiment which began in 1932 was a promise of health care to 600 black share-croppers who unwillingly and unknowing were injected with the syphilis virus that allowed to take its full course until their deaths. James Marion Sims, the founder of modern gynecology, made his strides at the cost of enslaved black women whom he would test, do studies with, and operate on, all without any form of anesthesia. Sims had the understanding that black women did not feel pain to the point that he operated on one 17 year old slave woman 30 times. The black community has suffered human testing and mutilation from the very people who promised to take care of them. Why do you think it is so difficult for many in the Black community to trust anyone in the medical field?

We have a pattern of fear when it comes to health-care, and we have a fear of pain. It is part of a pattern that we all must look at in our lives.

I Hurt!

We hurt!

When we hurt, we have this willingness to believe anything our caregivers tell us even if we do not agree. We must stop! If we feel we are not being heard and respected, we need to take our business elsewhere. Our health and our lives depend on it.

During my treatment for cancer, one of my oncologists felt that it was best to keep the fact that I had a second cancer from me until I was almost complete with treatment from the first cancer.

In the process, I relocated to live with my friend in NC who was a nurse, and I needed to find a new oncologist. You can imagine my surprise when he told me of the second cancer that had been there all along. I at once wrote to my first oncologist and advised him of my anger and pain at the fact that he had made a decision that was not his to do. No one had the right to decide what I could or could not handle but me. I urged him to think, going forward, more about his patients and a bit less about the chemical makeup of the care. We all need to ask for what we need and find someone who understands that need.

Many women die of breast cancer each year because they don't have an annual checkup. We have allowed the outside world to determine our value and worth, and it is time for us to take that back. WOMEN'S EMPOWERMENT! We can no longer sit silently and pretend that we are not afraid. It is now time to take the steps needed to change your life. More men die of prostate cancer due to the fact that they are unwilling to have an annual checkup. Men don't get sick and men don't die because they are the "providers" for the family.

Each of us has our make-believe stories that we tell ourselves to help us feel better until we don't, and when we feel pain, then we make up another set of stories altogether. Herein lies the premise of this book. When we begin to hurt, we must go within and find the willingness to look for the answers to what is causing the pain and what we can do to change it. It was on my first journey with cancer that I learned this lesson all too well.

Many of us think that pain is some form of punishment, and so much of what we hear from religion today echoes that all too well: good/bad, right/wrong, abundance/lack. The fact is: each of them is part of the same thing. My favorite example is give/receive. It took me the longest time to understand that one. You can't have one without the other. Most of my life I was taught that it is more blessed to give than receive. I was horrible at receiving when someone gave me a gift. I didn't know what to do. It was awkward, and most often the person giving the gift felt that I hated it.

In truth, I didn't know what to do with it; I didn't have a clue how to receive. Learning how to receive has been my greatest life lesson. Once I learned how to receive, I fully understood the joyous part of giving and the full reciprocity of how it works. No one had ever taken the time to tell me the difference between giving and receiving and how it is part of the same whole. You can't have one without the other. To be open to giving, you must have the openness within yourself to receive what someone has to give to you. If not, it is impossible for you to give anyone anything in love and have it fully received. It was through the pain of my unwillingness to receiving, that I found the will to look at myself intently. That I was able to find what needed to change within myself, and the willingness to do so. That is one of the many lessons I learned from my first cancer experience. I could have chosen to make it about bitterness, anger, and pain, but instead I choose to EMBRACE the lessons in my life and move forward.

For me, the pain has shown me where I was resisting the lesson.
Our bodies are amazing instruments of love, and we discount them every day.

We diminish them continually, saying things to ourselves like "stupid,"
"fat," "ugly," "lazy,"… and we wonder why our bodies don't support us.
When we hurt, it is a message from our body that we have missed when it
spoke to us in a softer, gentler, level. I always ask people to sit in silence
and listen. Meditation is a wonderful practice, and I love it; yet, silence is
different. Silence is where we sit and listen to what the universe wants to
say to us. When I say, "the universe," I mean all of existence. Can you
imagine that from the beginning of time until this moment wants to
communicate with you? Of course it does, because you are a part of it, and
it is all of you. That is why when we sit in silence and listen, we become
connected to every answer that has ever been, and it is all there deep within
us.

Example: *Silence*

*What is "being silent," and how does it help you find the wisdom within
yourself? Unlike other practices that have you focus on position,
chanting, or how well you do the training, silence asks that you have a
willingness to listen, with the intent to hear and remember who you are.
Silence is about trusting the whisper you hear in your heart over the
noise you hear in your head. Each of us remembers that we are part of a
greater whole. It is in the sacred silence that I bring any concern, worry,
fear, hope, desire, intent, and wish, and I know that it is being heard by a
greater consciousness. I have no need to plead or pray. I simply listen to
what the silence has to say. You will understand and know what the
silence is saying and communicating with you, much like the roots of a
tree commune with the branches and the sun. One song, many
frequencies.*

If you find that your mind is busy or tends to wonder, you can simply give it a job. Tell it to feel you hands and feet. Our minds are multidimensional, therefore very active. Once you honor your mind, you will find that it quiets down, and you will find that silence can give you all the answers you will ever need.

Once I began to listen to the silence and embrace my inner wisdom, my life began to change. I embraced each life lesson and moved forward. Please understand that some of them were more difficult than others, but whenever I needed strength, I knew where to find it.

I found that not only did the pain release, but so did the tension, fear, and anxiety that I had been holding onto as well. Making the decision that I no longer wanted to live in pain, fear, anger, regret, anxiety, lack, shame…you name it… was my first step to a new life. I have a life I had never dreamed possible because I had never seen myself as anything other than a victim.

Most of my adult time, I lived a dual life. In my business life, I was a leader, top of my game. I was Number 1 or nothing at all. I needed everyone to see me as the best. It was all about how people saw me. I wore the best clothes, had the most beautiful apartment in one of "those luxurious buildings" in the Oakland Bay area. When I talked to myself, I was demeaning and cruel. I realized that much of my adult life was tied up in how I looked to the outside world, and no matter how much I tried, I still believed I was worthless. When someone tells you,

"You are the lowest, most degrading thing on the face of the earth, and you are not my son," that has an impact on your life.

You can forgive it, heal from it, yet you can never forget it! It is something that is attached to you, if you answer to it. It affects your worth and value until you heal it within yourself.

I realized that at a deep and abiding level, I felt like garbage that had been discarded. I played that out over and over again in my life. I put a welcome mat at my door and invited everyone in, with the hope that if they could love me, it would prove that I was indeed lovable. What it often proved was that I had a lack of judgment, and I would usually be taken advantage of. Most often I felt as though I was garbage and I had no worth or value. On the rare occasion that I would meet someone that was kind and loving, I would find myself proving them wrong and unworthy of their love, often driving them away because I was unworthy of something so good, or I was incapable of allowing in love at all. I would often call myself stupid, lazy, and irresponsible. I would often have thoughts about myself that I was terrible with money, even though I was managing a multi-million dollar division of a Fortune 500 company. From the outside, I appeared to have everything together, while on the inside, my world was in utter chaos and falling apart. It was at this moment that I knew that "I was hurting and I no longer wanted to hurt anymore."

I had been a part of a new thought community in California. The spiritual leader, Dr. Elouise Oliver, had inspired me to go within and look at what I was saying to myself and about myself. Each week, Rev. E would have us recite an affirmation about taking dominion in our lives. In all my years of religion and spirituality, I had never found a place that asked me to go within and realize that my dominion and The Dominion were the same.

My soul began to come alive as I began to realize that all things were interconnected, much like when we planted beans in milk cartons as children in elementary school. We learned the connection between the earth and the seed. What you plant is what you will receive.

I was perplexed, worried, and hopeful, all at the same time. Confused, as this was something that I had never heard before, and somehow I knew it was the path to freedom. Worried, because at the moment I knew how I felt about myself, and thinking if The Divine and I were indeed interconnected, boy was I/IT in deep trouble! Hopeful, because, for the first time in my lifetime, I did indeed see a glimmer of hope, and my heart came alive with desire. I wanted more from my life. I began to listen to what I was saying to myself, not out of judgment, but as a silent witness to become aware so that I could have the courage to begin my transformation in my personal life.

I realized that I had been living my personal life from a state of lack and that I was living my professional life in abundance, so I chose to change that first. I was living from the outside in, and I wanted to live from the inside out! I was living from pay check to pay check. As someone who was making six-figures, I knew I wanted to change my lack mentality in my personal life. When you live in lack, it doesn't matter how much money you make because it is never enough, because it has a way of vanishing. I knew that to create a new life, I had to change my consciousness about who I AM and how I see abundance in my personal life. I could no longer live this way, nor did I want to. The pain of living in this state of consciousness was so great that I became willing to take a new path. "I was hurting, and I didn't want to hurt any longer."

Little did I know at that time that this emotional pain, along with the self-hatred, had been eating away at my life for so long unattended that within a few months I would be diagnosed with lymphoma and renal cancer. Years of self-hatred and fear had created so much self-loathing that I continued to shove deep within until it created dis-ease.

Within months of my decision to change, I had help from the universe in the form of cancer. "I was hurting, and I didn't want to hurt any longer." Not only had the pain become so great that I had become willing to change, it had become so real that I had two choices: change or die! I chose to change. It was a real life-changer when they told me that I had stage 4 lymphoma, that I could die, and I needed to get my affairs in order. At that moment, I became aware that it was time to make some changes that could affect my life forever and not just for the moment. It no longer mattered what "you," the outside world thought of me. It was about clearing out and cleaning up anything that was going to kill me. I was hurting, and I was going to die if I didn't change. Most of us don't get this kind of wake-up call. For me, it was just what I needed. Pain usually is the perfect stimulant to get us going in some direction. We don't see it at the time, yet when we look back on it, we know that it was the motivation that we needed at the time to move us forward.

Whatever it is that you want to change in your life: Do it now! We always talk about how we felt that gentle nudge to go on the trip, visit our family, tell a friend how much we loved them, and we didn't listen. And then… the unexpected happened, and we no longer have a choice. Don't wait for the pain to show you how.

Don't wait for the fire, the accident, or the death to tell the people in your life how much you love them. Now is the only moment that we have, which is why it is called the present. Unwrap it with love, and live fully in it.

Example: Sacred Silence

Ten minutes in the morning and before bed.

To embrace this practice into my life in a meaningful way, I found that it was essential to do this twice a day. I enjoy sacred silence once in the morning and once before bed. When I enjoy sacred silence in the morning, it allows me to connect with my highest self, first thing before going out into the day. When I enjoy sacred silence in the evening, it allows me to release any conditions, concerns, and patterns that I may have picked up during the day, release it, and once again return to my highest self before going to bed. In this example, you will see how I enjoy sacred silence: I lie flat on a mat, blanket, place my hands on my lower (abdomen for men) (chest or heart for women.) The point of the exercise is to open our minds. Listen with the intent to hear without the need to respond. Our minds are often so busy with thoughts and chatter that when we can spend ten minutes twice a day in sacred silence listening for inner wisdom, we open our souls to the universal guidance and a path that is best for each of us. When we set aside ten minutes twice a day, it allows us to grow a life that is productive, full, vibrant, filled with love and abundance.

(Remember there is no set way to perform sacred silence; these are simple guidelines) Example: Silence Ten minutes in the morning and before bed.

NOTES

Step 2

One of the greatest gifts I ever received was the gift of friendship from a friend named Laurie F. I was new to Huntsville, Alabama, and I wanted some friends of my own. I was in a new relationship, and I knew that if it was going to work, I couldn't rely on him for everything. I met Laurie at church, and we visited a couple of times. She asked if I wanted to meet and talk about being friends.

I thought to myself, "Yes, I would love to be your friend."

When I arrived, she thanked me for coming, and we talked for a moment. Then she said, "I would like to interview you for friendship!" I asked, "What?" I had never had that happen before. She talked to me about the importance of knowing what my strength was and questioned how I handled anger. She stated that, "Every relationship, regardless of what they are, will have moments when you will need to be strong and when you will be weak. It will also have moments of joy and moments of anger, and if we are going to be great friends, we need to know how we are going to handle that before we start this."

Friendship Interview

I was stunned!

Not in a way that put me off. In a way that I was in my 30's, and no one had ever spoken to me like this before. I had created relationships all my life, and NO ONE had ever put that much intention into anything with me. I had spent the previous year dealing with sexual abuse in my childhood, and the rape when I was 19 years old, so I knew that everything she was saying to me was indeed the truth. Here was this person in front of me loving me in a way unlike anyone had ever loved me before, and we hadn't even decided "if" we were going to be friends!

Here are the questions she asked of me:

  *What do you bring to the table?

  *What are the areas in your life you want to work on?

  *How do you handle conflict?

  *How do you ask for what you need?

  *What do you expect from me?

  *What do you want from this friendship?

These were not questions you can answer on the spot, nor would you want to. When we met again in two weeks to discuss our answers, I realized that these are questions everyone should answer for every relationship in their lives. Not only did I build a wonderful, loving, life-changing relationship with my friend Laurie F, but that became the foundation of my work from that day forward.

It was a clear and precise way to help others understand my boundaries and ask for what I needed in a relationship. It was a step in the direction up the ladder to freedom.

Each time when I have taken the time to interview a friend, I have never been disappointed. The moments I overlook it or chose not to invest in myself, the cost has been high. The point here is that you're building a life in which you are surrounding yourselves with people that will stand in your greatness. Part of having a loving, joyous, fulfilling life is understanding where to invest and when to let go.

Am I willing to change the way I have been living so that I never have to feel hurt like this again?

How much time do we spend getting to know each other before we get married? What do you need to get married in the United States: a couple of days, a blood test, and two legal-aged adults, if that? We spend more time getting out of relationships once we are in pain than we do building healthy ones along the way. Why is that? We have been taught to believe in love at first sight. Happily-ever-after and all the hocus pocus from the fairy tale stories we were told as children which created a great deal of the hidden beliefs that we live by today.

*The knight in shining armor coming to save me.
*The damsel in distress who requires rescue.
*Princess (virgin) more beautiful than all the maidens in the world.

We will meet the handsome prince, fall in love, and live happily-ever-after, or we will find the girl of our dreams, and she will be a virgin in need of rescue, and we will help her, and she will fall in love with us, and we will live happily-ever-after. What happens when that story breaks down? What happens when that is an untruth? What happens when that hurts?

Most often when we meet someone, we find that it is our hormones that lead the way, and we can't see the forest for the trees. We don't know if they have cab fare home, and, to be honest, we don't care! We are in love, and that is all that matters. Everything about them is perfect, and there is nothing that anyone can tell us that would make a difference. We all know we have been there; sometimes, more than once. Your best friend tries their best to point out even the tiniest of flaws, and you claim they are jealous or/and they want them for themselves, only to find a few weeks, or years, later, when you are in pain, that you are furious with your friends for not telling you the truth about who this person was.

Change happens when we are ready and not one moment before.

Change usually occurs for one of these three reasons:

    Friction: *Divorce, Lawsuit, Argument*
    Situation: *Loss of job/New Job, Buy/Sell house*
    Pain: *Death, Illness, Disease, Natural disaster*

As a general rule, we don't jump into change for the heck of it.

I have a willingness to change

Am I willing to change?

Am I willing to change the way I am living my life?

Am I willing to change the people in my life to have a better life experience?

Am I willing to spend less time with my family if they trigger me?

Am I willing to change the way I eat, live, and love in order to have a more loving life?

Am I willing to change my spending habits in order to have a new home?

People in my life have two choices: they can step up or step off. I am not saying that who they are is good or bad, right or wrong. I am merely saying I need more from life, and if they want to be a part of my life, I now know what I need from this point going forward. If anyone is unwilling to meet the new standard, they have no business in my life. I, too, must understand how vital this is for my life going forward. If not, I will remain on step 2 for the rest of my life. Most importantly, I have to be willing to let anyone or anything go if I am going to grow. Once we see some change in our lives, we often relax and find ourselves back at step 1 one only to realize that this time, as much as we would like to blame someone else, we are fully aware that we have created this situation for ourselves. We often repeat steps1 and 2 over and over again, thinking: I can help others grow with me, or they will change if they love me. We have this fear that we want to belong, and yet we fear we don't belong to anything. We are so convinced that we live in an "I vs. them" mentality. We begin to believe that we are un-lovable and that no one would dare connect with us.

We fear it is impossible for us to find love, so we live at step 1 allowing anyone and everyone to wander into our lives, believing it is better to have "something, which is better than nothing at all."

When others come into our lives and ask us to diminish ourselves so that they are comfortable, we become a doormat in their lives, somewhere for them to wipe their dirty feet. How dare they come into your life and request this of you! You must stop that behavior. You must live your authentic life and allow them to do the same.

You must say: "I will no longer diminish what The Divine created so that you feel okay!"

NO!

That is your cue to remove yourself and allow them to continue on their path, understanding that it is perfectly fine for them to journey on without you. You do not need to allow anyone into your life who will ask you in any way to diminish who "You Are"! You realize they are asking you to diminish The Divine within, which created everything in the universe. You now realize, "You are" divine. You release anyone who cannot recognize that within you now. You bless them, and you let them go.

What does it mean to have a willingness to change? For the longest time, I loved to play with this idea. I would diet, fast, do without sex, only to find myself, in the end, hating myself more, knowing that the universe had known the truth all along. Here is the secret: the universe is always watching.

Most of us have a mobile device today. 90% of them can tell us where we are, and, if we ask, they can tell us where the nearest place to eat, get gas, and purchase anything - whatever our hearts desire. A great many of us have in-home devices as well. Therefore, we are never without assistance. Here is the funny thing in all of this: we have never been without assistance. From the beginning of time, we believed we were separate and not interconnected, because that is what we were led to believe. However, if we were to tap into the silence and listen, we can understand our connection to everything within creation.

Now, how do we start living into step 2 in our lives?

Take a moment and go outside to the front of your house, apartment, or wherever you are living. Take a piece of paper and pen or your mobile device, as you will be taking some notes.

> *How welcoming does it look?*
> *Do you have a welcome mat?*
> *Do you have a deadbolt?*
> *How many steps do you have to the entrance?*
> *Would you want to visit yourself?*
> *How many people have keys to your home?*

Ok, let's go back inside and start working. When we begin the transformation of our lives, we want to start with the outside because that is where everyone is looking. When we do this, it never really lasts because we can't keep up appearances. However, we are going to use all of this information for our good in this chapter. To change who we are on the outside, we need to look at who we're giving access to in our lives.

Why?

It tells us what we think we are worth.

Most often we will make the outside of our homes look warm, and inviting so that others will want to come in and visit with us, or we will make our homes look ugly and unkept so that others will stay away because we feel unlovable. We all have patterns and behaviors, and the more we can look at those and have the willingness to change those, the more we can grow and evolve in our daily lives. Most of these patterns developed within the first five to seven years of our lives.

In the last chapter, we talked about pain and receiving. Many of us don't want to grow or evolve unless we have to. Before I met my husband, I had been celibate for a year, because, all of my life, sex had been about sexual pleasure for the other person or about me living in a state of numbness due to sexual abuse within my own life. That became the gateway to cancer, which allowed me to take a hard look at what was eating me. Through this work, I've done a great deal to open my heart, which allowed me to be open to receiving love.

I want to share with you a story how my heart opened as it had never done so before. it was an experience with my beloved husband. No matter what is going on in our lives, we always find time to talk and make time together. If we need some quiet time, we give it to each other. If we need a date night, we make sure we plan a special evening together. I would gladly go through my life again, all of it, cancer, too, to find my Tony. I remember the moment that my heart opened as it never had before.

I had been in a great deal of pain, my appendix had ruptured, and I needed emergency surgery. It was late in the evening when I came out of emergency surgery. My beloved sat up all night in a chair next to my hospital bed holding my hand so I could sleep peacefully through the night. That one moment changed my life forever. Never had anyone loved me so deeply! I vowed at that moment to open my heart and EMBRACE life, no matter the risk, regardless of the pain, simply because Love was worth the risk.

I have learned from the pain that the embrace of love is more vibrant and full than I could have imagined, for they are part of the same whole. I now look for love at every turn and focus on love with the knowledge that it will always lead me home.

How did I begin this shift in my thinking?

I realize now that my heart had been closed for a long time, even though I had always been a very loving person. I had a belief that if I loved you enough and pleased you sexually that you would love me and never leave. I believed that someone would come in and love the unlovable boy. I would give keys to everyone I loved with the hope they would all stay.

Who has access to your life and why?

As a child who had suffered sexual abuse from age three to sixteen, and as a teen who at the age of eighteen was violated by rape, I knew all too well about giving the "wrong people" access to my life. When my parents found out that I was gay, they told me I was not their son. They informed me that my friends nor my presence were welcome in their home. Please hear me when I say this is not about blame; this is about accountability.

For me to do my work, I needed to look at what I was "doing my best not to feel." All of my life, everyone had access to my life. We were not allowed to close the doors and lock them. We didn't even have locks on them. I was bullied every day at school, from the third grade until I graduated, for being different. I was called "sissy," "queer," "faggot"; I was shoved, pushed, and called every name you can imagine. Back then, in the deep South, it wasn't called "bullying," it was "boys being boys." Most of my life, I felt like a welcome mat, and my job was to please everyone so that they were happy, and if they weren't happy, my life was hell.

I did my best to be the perfect boy in my family home. When I was 15, my mama found out I was gay. It was at that moment that my secret was no longer a secret, and I was the one who had broken her heart. It was the first time in my life I saw mama cry hysterically, and I made it happen. I was no longer her baby; I was now the unlovable boy with a horrible secret - the secret of shame I must keep from my father. I was the only thing on earth that "God" could not love.

No matter what they had taught me as a child, from that moment forward, in their eyes, I became the unlovable boy. Within the year, my daddy found out the secret from my brother, and suddenly I was no longer welcomed there. I began my quest for love and my desire to be numb. I had years of experience at pleasing other people sexually, so I found it easy to find people who wanted "sexual love." I had blond hair and blue eyes and was barely 17 years old. Painful as it was, love had never lasted because in my heart and mind I knew who I was, the unlovable boy. When we hold onto a belief, it will continue to show up in our lives again and again until we unpack it and heal it.

This hatred that I had for myself as the unlovable boy kept growing inside with each relationship. If I chose a bad boy, it was punishment for being the unlovable boy. If I found a good man who wanted to love me, it wasn't long before I found a way to reveal myself as unlovable and unworthy of their love. This pattern would show up again and again, sometimes in six months, sometimes in two years. It always showed up, for it was my belief system about who I was. Time and time again I would hurt, tell my story, still blaming the "other guy," unwilling or not wanting to notice the pattern or the fact that there was one common denominator, and I was it. It was not until I heard the word cancer that I stopped long enough to understand what the universe wanted me to hear.

As I sat there in the silence, I knew the answers, each of them, as they came to me. It was as if each answer had been a part of me all along and I was too afraid to acknowledge them or too scared to honor the parts of myself that each of them represented.

I had to change.

When we EMBRACE change, we are growing. We are moving the boundaries in our lives as we embark on a new life. One of my favorite acronyms for CHANGE is:

"I"

Can

Handle

A

New

Growth

Experience

I often say, "*I CHANGE!*" It is the realization that "I AM" willing to handle a new growth experience in my life. We are no longer living at Step 1 where everyone has access to our lives; we have stepped up one step, which means that everyone that we knew at ground level no longer has access to our lives. I change, and the world around me will change as well. As above, so below. As within, so without. I had heard these phrases in the spiritual community that I had been attending, and it was at this moment they were beginning to come alive within my life. I could no longer live my old life and expect something new.

> *"You can never solve a problem on the level*
> *from which it was created."*
> *Albert Einstein*

When we look at a seed, it might be easy to think what the possibilities within this tiny capsule are. Therein lies the secret of all life. Within each of us, just as within the seed, is the same capability that exists within all of the universes. For within each seed is the concept, idea, desire, or intent to become anything that the seed desires to become. For the seed has implanted within itself the makeup and intention to grow into a bean, tomato, apple,,,, the list is endless.

Once we plant the seed, it has the understanding to release the creation within. It must undergo a transformation of a significant nature in which it will no longer resemble its current makeup to bring the desired intent into manifestation. With the warmth (heat/pain/contrast) of the earth and the rays of the sun, the seed explodes with intention and begins the creation process by pushing its first beanstalk up through the ground.

All of this is part of the miracle of intention and is within us all. When pain, anger, suffering, or what we know as contrast comes into our lives, it is always for one purpose: to help us grow, just like the seed.

NOTES

Step 3

Here I was at the edge of creation with the understanding that I could create anything I desired, and I knew that I was responsible for what I created. What was it going to be? All of this had come at a pivotal moment in my life. Being a New Thought Metaphysician, I knew some basic concepts about transformation. One concept is: to see the change, I had to believe in what it was I wanted to see. If I wanted to have an abundant life, I had to believe it was possible for me. I knew that I could change my hidden belief into something new once I knew what that hidden belief was. As a Metaphysician, it was all about what I was putting into the universe (soil) as to what I got back. I began to listen to what I was saying about my finances and myself. I would hear words like "stupid. You can't rub two nickels together to make a dime! Money doesn't grow on trees!" I realized that these statements were not my truth as I was one of the top salespeople for the company and I was responsible for training 6-10 new sales associates as well. A few months earlier, I had wanted to change my financial wellbeing. As part of that, I noticed that I made millions of dollars for the companies that I worked for, and yet I was living paycheck to paycheck. I made a six-figure income that was vanishing into thin air due to a belief about my worth and value. For me to change it, I spent two weeks observing my conversation with myself and about myself. I also asked my friends what books they suggested I read about abundance. Within two weeks, I had amassed a great deal of research on my behavior and speech. It was my voice, yet the message I was hearing were the words I had heard my parents say constantly:

"You can't rub two nickels together to make a dime."

Please hear me. I am not blaming my parents. What I want each of us to recognize at this moment is that most of our patterns of behavior come from our parents or someone we love before the age of seven. Not all of those patterns serve us well into our adult life, as we will discover. We can erase them and replace them with new ones that serve us better. In this case, I attached meaning to the message that my parents said and took it in to be my truth. We all do this in our lives. That is the point of looking at our hidden beliefs to see if they serve us well. If not, replace them with something that does. My parents grew up in a large family where every penny counted. Some of their money conversations reflected that. I want an abundance conversation that indicates something different. To change that, I had to be aware when the old messages were playing so that I could STOP it and replace it with something new.

I-CHANGE!

I tested that theory, and it worked rather quickly. If I wanted love in my life, I had to believe it was possible for me. It was much like planting the bean that I planted when I was a child in elementary school. Did I think it was going to grow, or did I believe it was going to die?

Whatever I believed was what would manifest in my life. What I put into the universe (soil) is what I was going to get back.

I began to see something of the utmost importance in my life and affairs. Up until that moment, I had been blaming everyone else for what had gone wrong in my life, when, in fact, it was me who had been planting one thing in the universal soil of life expecting something else.

What I was collecting was the bounty of my harvest. It was a moment of awakening! If I didn't like what I was harvesting, I needed to change what I was planting.

It was indeed time for a change.

One of my favorite books is Louise Hays' *You Can Heal Your Life*. In it, she talks about the power of affirmations. I have read this book many times. Learning to use affirmations as well as intentions are invaluable tools in our growth to self-awareness and self-love.

Validating the self

I began asking myself some logical questions:

If I am so bad with money, why am I a top sales associate in X company?

If I am bad with money, would X company allow me to train new associates?

No!

I had these messages that were hidden deep within my life, running and ruling my finances. Now, to move to the next step! I needed and wanted to change them. I decided to play a game. I knew the old messages and what they were saying. What message would I like to put in their place?

I sat in silence for a few days asking the universe for the perfect Affirmation/Mantra to fill the void. Here is what I was given: "There is always enough!" For the following six weeks, anytime I heard one of the "old" messages come up, I would say the word "STOP!" and replace it with the "new" Mantra!

Saying a Mantra.

Example:

(Mantra: a statement or slogan repeated frequently.)

(Old message) You can't rub two nickels together to make a dime!

STOP!

(New Mantra) There is always enough!

In step 3, you begin finding all the pieces and parts of yourself that you love. Stay here until it works. You repetitively affirm all the things that you love about who you are and release the things that no longer work. Many people feel that after a while they become bored and tired of tracking and monitoring their thoughts of what they are thinking and saying. My intent is to remind each of us that, much like going to the gym, when we exercise, the muscles become stronger. When we stop, they become weak and lose any memory of flexibility, and we often fall into old patterns of behavior.

Living in a new way takes work, diligence, and we may think, over time, it is not worth the effort. We forget the pain we endured before we climbed the steps to step 3. Being lax in judgment will find us at step 1 - hurting, wondering how we got there again. The only difference would be that we now know we are responsible for the hidden belief pattern. Only you will know when you are ready to move forward, and only you can prepare for your future. The desire to change must be greater than the desire to stay the same. Like a plane taking flight, the thrust of taking off must be greater than the gravity holding it to the ground.

At this moment in our lives, we begin to feel better. Our lives are better than they were in the past. As we move upward on the steps, we look better, and others are starting to take note of it. Old playmates and old playthings will come knocking on your door from step1 and step 2, wanting you to give them access into your life again. Guilting you, perhaps telling you that you are different and that you don't love them anymore. It is important that you honor who you are and that you stay the course realizing that if they want to join you, they can step up to where you are rather than you stepping down to where they are. I urge you to stay here at step 3 as long as you need to get a clear understanding of how to honor and affirm the person you are becoming. Learn how to notice where the weeds from the past want to creep in through the cracks and how you can close those off. Notice who in your life is a trigger and plan your interaction with them. If you cannot release them from your life entirely, have an escape plan in the event you are triggered and need to leave. Learning to love yourself is of the utmost importance as you journey forward into self-worth

Learning to love who you are.

How do you start to love yourself? We must first understand that we are talking about love verses affection. Few of us know the difference between the two. What most of us are talking about when we talk about love is affection. I have affection for you. Affection is something that I can give and take away based on an event: I am angry or frustrated, or you didn't do what I asked you to do. That is affection.

Love, however, is unconditional. I may not like your behavior, yet my love for you is always the same. It is my desire in this step to give some examples of how we can shift from affection to love, not only for ourselves, but for those we love in our daily lives. The point of this step is to find the part of yourself that you like. What are your best qualities that you want to bring forward in life? Before you say, "I don't have any!", everyone has something that they do better than anyone else. It is our job to go within, find that, and bring it forward.

I have a talent for decorating and organizing things. I didn't see that as anything special for the longest time. I would make sure my apartment, closets, and cabinets were in the best order. Because it made it easy for me to tell my friends where to find things when they were visiting me. I could say precisely where something was due to my organizational skills. Soon I was helping my friends with their homes as well. I loved putting closet organizers together and making the most out of closet spaces. I took that skill along with my design skills and turned it into an interior design degree which I enjoyed for many years.

I still have clients who seek my design skills today.

Even though I enjoy it, my passion has moved in other directions. In life, we find certain qualities that we love about ourselves, develop them, and allow them to lead us to the next step, which we follow until the next step appears.

For most of my life, I was great with my decor'. I could put anything together and make it look good. I could take what people had in their homes and rearrange it and make it look like something new: take a rug from one room and move it to another room, paint a wall here and there, and voila! You have transformed people's lives, well, their homes at least! I knew I wanted more from my life than helping people update where they were living. I wanted to help them rearrange their souls, their inner lives. To do that, I had to do that for myself first. My life looked good from the outside, beautiful things in all the right places. I wanted to rearrange my insides to the point that I loved or at least liked who I was. I wanted change! I knew I was ready and willing to try almost anything.

Within six weeks of doing this exercise daily, I had transformed my household finances. I had created a savings account. As well as invested in a matching 401K with the Fortune company with the money that I was able to put aside. I was transforming the way I looked at money, my finances, and how money looked at me. So much of our lives we think we don't have what we want due to the fact someone or something is standing in our way. What we often don't notice is that the thing is us. Over the years I have continued my work with my mantras on abundance, and I am pleased to say that from that point onward I have been abundantly blessed.

It was that breakthrough that made me question a great deal in my life. Where else were these messages hiding in my life?

What other parts of my life had they infiltrated and taken over
without my knowledge? One of the greatest quests in my life was love. In
fact, I think this has been my greatest lifelong quest. It started with the
not-so-hidden belief that I was unlovable because of the fact that I was gay.
Being gay in the Deep South in a very Christian home is most likely the
worst thing that can happen to you. I knew I was gay at a very young age
and was bullied every day of my childhood and teenage life as a result of
it. Add in sexual abuse and the fear that the one ally that I had, my mama,
would one day find out and hate me. I hid everything hoping that I would
be safe. Secrets, all the secrets: sexually pleasing the ones that no one
knows about, and hiding from the ones that are not to know. Hiding from
my family due to the fact I didn't want them to know what everyone was
calling me at school. I did my best to be a perfect child so that my family
would love me. I didn't break the rules. I did my best to make everyone
happy. I wanted everyone to love me.

The only issue with hidden things is they cause problems, as we learned
from the exercise above. I realized that although I had been to therapy to
deal with sexual abuse, I still hadn't dealt with all the hidden beliefs that
were hanging around that created the sexual abuse in the first place: the
need to be loved at any cost. What were the messages I was saying about
myself around love? Dare I ask? Dare I listen? "You are fat. No one wants
you. You are unlovable. Who would love you?"… and the list goes on. I
knew I had a great deal of work to do. How and where do I start?

Example:

(Old message) I am the unlovable boy.

STOP!

(New Mantra) I love and approve of myself.

Example:

(Old message) I don't deserve to be in love.

STOP!

(New Mantra) I am worthy of love!

Mirror work.

I had done "mirror work" a million times or more: standing there looking at myself and telling myself how much I love myself, only to move on through my day realizing I didn't mean any of it at all. Affection vs. love. Affection is something that I can give and take away based on an event. Love, however, is unconditional. Affection can be removed with a whim, while love is constant. I wanted to find love in my life. It was time for me to change how I looked at love and how I looked at myself. Within the following six months, I received my first diagnosis of cancer. The doctor said I had Lymphoma; it is a fast-growing cancer, stage 4. I had to organize and pack everything I owned and put it into boxes, because the life I had grown accustomed to was going away.

The penthouse apartment, my lovely job, and the way people looked at me from the outside in were all going away. The most considerable change of all was how I looked at myself.

One of my favorite things in my penthouse was a full-length mirror I have had for years. After receiving the news from the doctor about cancer, I drove home to my lovely penthouse where I turned off all the music and lights. I sat there in the darkness of what I call "the void of the unknown." In a loud voice, I stated: "You have my attention! I am listening." As I sat there in the void of the unknown waiting for an answer here is what I heard "I have you; all is well!" It was in that moment I realized I had never been alone! From the beginning of time, and I would never be alone again. No matter where the journey may lead, and no matter if I took it by myself, I was never alone. I understood from that moment forward that I was surrounded by everyone who had ever gone before me. Every teacher, healer, guide, mentor, sacred soul, ancestor, who had ever loved and honored me just as I am without condition or judgment, was there standing with me at that moment in time. I had a journey to take, a journey of love. As I sat there releasing a lifetime of self-hatred, fear, anger, bitterness, unworthiness, I began to understand that I needed this moment to help me heal. It was not about punishment; it was about restoration.

I went to the mirror and took off my clothes one piece at a time, because I wanted to honor myself as you do someone you love. I was no longer numb or fulfilling someone else's fantasy. I could see a lovable boy who had grown into a good-looking, handsome man. I saw the depth of the ocean as I looked in my eyes. I saw the strength of Atlas as I looked at my broad shoulders who had for a lifetime been carrying a heavy load.

I looked at my body covered with hair, and I saw the heritage of my Scottish and Norwegian ancestors I then realized that regardless of whom I choose to love, I had become a man of honor who no longer needed to hold his head in shame. My loving heart was in love for the first time with who I saw looking back at me. I took a moment to gather myself and my emotions, and I grabbed the camera and took pictures of the one I love! Today, those pictures still inspire me and remind me to let go of anything that is no longer needed and to always love who you are.

I had taken steps to clear the path for a new life, much like you would for a new crop.

Throughout much of our lives, we think that once we have had a breakthrough, our work is complete. We think we don't have any more work to do. We can sit by the fire and sing Kumbaya songs, when, in fact, the work is just beginning. Growing up in a farming community, I learned a great deal. There is a lot of work that goes into having a farm. My parents had a couple of acres of land where we planted a garden and raised pigs and cows each year for our family to live on during the winter months. To grow something new, you need to clear the land of what has been planted before; otherwise, what you're planting doesn't stand a chance of producing. It is also a good idea for the soil to be "turned over" for the new crop. When you think about it, we have to do the same thing in our personal lives as well. We have to clear away the things that no longer serve us in our lives. Then we turn the soil by sitting in silence and falling in love with who we are; clearing away any hidden beliefs that are causing us harm. Then we begin planting love.

The number one thing that people talk with me about is their family, friends, and loved ones. How do I bring them along with me into this new garden?

 My question to them is, "Will that create any different experience than what you had in the past?" It is difficult to say goodbye to people, places, and things that we had affection for so long. At this point in the steps is where a lot of people may stop and return to step 1 because they need to feel more pain again. Your life is better than it has been for most of your life and your old friends from steps 1 - 3 are now want what you have. The moment you open the door to them and allow them access into your life, they will take what they want and once again vanish into thin air until they need you again. It is necessary that everyone take the steps for themselves; there are NO SHORT CUTS! You see things more clearly now and realize that as much as you want to help them to improve themselves, you must stop your pattern of behavior. It is time to allow the universe to support them the way it did with you.

Here is the other option:

What if?

What if you change your life and fall in love with who you are so profoundly that you permit them to do the same. What if you live your life so boldly that they can't stand it, and they have to find this path for themselves, only to discover they have to love themselves - which means you both are on the same path? What if you love who you are so much you realize they are on their path, which is perfect for them, and they will arrive when it is right for them? What if they are perfect just as they are?

Are you willing to move forward and let go? Are you ready to find what you need to set your life free and allow others to do the same? Are you willing to be the trailblazer you came here to be? Now is your moment, and this is your time! Only you can make this decision, and only you can clean your path. Once you've cleared it and prepared the soil, what you put in it is up to you.

What do I want in my life going forward? Am I willing to care for it daily, nurture it with love?

Like the exercise we did at the beginning of the step; it is important to listen to what you say, think, and feel about yourself daily. One of the best ways I know to explain this is, if you plant an apple tree expecting oranges, you are going to be disappointed.

However, that is what a lot of us do every day. We say again and again, "I want love," and the hidden messages we think, speak, and feel are that "I am not worthy, I am ugly, I am fat…" And that is why we cleared the path for planting something new. From time to time, we will find that old patterns want to resurface and weed themselves back into our new garden. It is essential to listen, look, and be aware of our emotions and how we feel.

Example:

   Hidden belief: You are unlovable.

   STOP

   New Mantra: I am worthy of love NOW.

If at any time we should find a weed growing in our garden, we should remove it at once and instantly fill it in with a new plant that we desire. Nature does not like a vacuum. If you leave one, the universe will fill it. That is why in the beginning we need to be vigilant of our thoughts, words, and deeds. If we have a thought that is not in alignment with what we have planted in our new garden, say "cancel" and think a thought that is in alignment with what you want. Before you take on anything new, ask if it is in alignment with your highest self. If so, move ahead. If not, stop and reassess your actions until you are in alignment with your new intentions. Are you living in alignment with what you want in your life? If not, why not?

Our community affirms: "That which we give out comes back heaped up and running over as part of our 'joyous giving.'" Joyous giving is the act of giving your financial gift or investments in a joyous way. The reason you are giving it is because it brings you JOY! It is a reminder that what we give is coming back in a joyous manner. No one is going to become a tattle tell and tell the universe what you have done. They don't "need to." The energy that we send out into the universe comes back to us. When we learn to love ourselves fully, no matter what others do, love is all we see, feel, and have around us, regardless of condition. No one is going to tell on you if you are not living in alignment with yourself. Remember as we move forward from this step going upward, we will no longer be able to go back to the place where we can blame others for our life being out of alignment. You have now taken full responsibility for your life, and all that happens to it. It would be like the farmer blaming the tomato seeds for not growing apples.

Responsibility! What you put into the universe is what you get back!

As within, so without.

As above, so below.

At this point, we learn to live the life we have dreamed of living. We know that whatever we put into the fertile (soil) of the universe, water it daily with thanksgiving, and do what is expected of us along the way, it will be made manifest. Whatever it may be, love, money, success, we plant it and care for it, and it will manifest. We have affirmed it, planted it, and we live with the expectation that it is on its way. Just like the bean we planted in primary school in the milk carton. We don't know how it works. We just know that it works. We are living a new life, and we love it.

Just like a garden, we have to nurture it daily. Once we know what we want, we make sure we are not planting anything other than that in our garden. Trust me when I say that everyone from steps one, two, and three, will do their best to get back into your gardens and sow seeds of their own. Remember: this is the step where you take responsibility for your life. Your life has changed: your finances, the way you look, and the way people look at you. Many find this a slippery step which can be the gateway back to step 1 and pain.

Step 4

Day to day life is finally feeling better, and any need to return to steps 1- 3 is completely due to planting one thing and expecting something else, and any hope of trying to bring others along before they are ready. We now understand that you cannot give a gift to anyone who is not yet prepared to receive it. There will be plenty of people who want to take the steps we have chosen who are unwilling to do the work. Any attempt to give it away for nothing requires that we return to step 1 and pain. Today you realize your worth and are now ready to step in a new direction that will elevate you one step higher toward freedom. You understand that Self-Worth will give you unlimited freedom and set you free from the need for outside validation, and that is a quest that you are ready to EMBRACE completely.

This step is about learning to validate who we are in such a way that we understand our worth wholeheartedly without the need for ego. We meet a great many people in life who feel the world revolves around them and need constant validation to support that. That is not at all what we are speaking about here. Often the ego's need for validation is driven by low self-worth. Our job in this step is to find any remnant of our hidden beliefs and move forward with the truth of who we know ourselves to be. The point of learning to give ourselves what we want is to understand our "worth and value."

Once we set a standard, we know instantly if that standard has been met or not.

My new standard: I am worthy of "Loving Relationship."

Example:
The man I am dating is cruel, belittles me, makes fun of my ideas, and he only calls when he is feeling sexual.

Key point: Moving between steps three and four is common.

I understand this is an exaggeration; I do, however, want to make this point very clear. As we find that we have lowered a standard in our lives, it is the realization that we have work to do. We now take responsibility for how it is showing in our lives. We look at the hidden belief and clear it up, and we once again set a new standard and move forward with the realization that we are stronger and wiser than before.

Once we are at this step, it is up to us to make sure who enters into our lives and that what they bring is what we want.

Once we set a standard, if we allow anyone to fall below that standard and enter our lives, from that point forward we have now established a new lower standard for entry into our lives. We have stepped back to a previous step along the journey. The reason we spend so much time on step 3 is because it allows us to do the clearing work that we require for a new life. It does us no good to clear the way for a new garden if we are only going to plant the same thing we removed. Being vigilant about our new standard is of the utmost importance, for it is the foundation of our new life.

Can you imagine having your home burglarized and how vulnerable you would feel?

You call a locksmith and have all the locks changed and get new keys.

You have a new standard in your life. Right?

Now, you give the new keys to the people who burglarized you because you   thought they were your friends.

Do I know what this person is bringing into my life? Have I interviewed them? Have I used the tools within my life to support my highest and best good?   Am I taking responsibility for who is walking through the threshold of my life? Have I removed the "welcome mat" that I once understood myself to be and replaced it with the understanding that I no longer have to allow everyone into my life with their expectation that I take care of their needs. I now have a new awareness in my life and now know my worth and my value. I also understand that if for any reason I lose sight of that understanding, it is up to me to repair it.

What do I do when I meet the person of my dreams, and the person likes me?

Embody who I AM!

It is easy when we meet someone special to want to fall back into our old beliefs. You have now created a new life; you are beginning to love who you are, and it can feel overwhelming. Can I keep this up? Do I deserve this? What if?

Those are the moments when our old ways of living try to creep into our new lives and do their best to dismantle it one thought at a time. Remember: nature dislikes a vacuum. Most of us are better at "not good enough" than at "excellent." When things are going great, we tend to ask how "we" can mess it up. That is the point of setting a standard and knowing who you are. You have worked to replace the hidden beliefs and created a new life by setting standards that support you. Who wouldn't love that? You have transformed your life and the way you live in it. You now realize that you have a creative, powerful, intelligent universe supporting you and that you can use it to create whatever you want. With that knowledge comes responsibility—a responsibility to be mindful of your actions, thoughts, words, and deeds. You now know that when you change your thoughts and deeds, you change your life.

Example:

I'm unlovable.

STOP

I AM worthy of love!

It is in moments such as this that you begin to realize you are creating the life you wish to live, and with that knowledge and power comes responsibility. If something or someone entered into your life that is unpleasing, you now have the tools at your disposal to release them from your life. There is no longer any need to live from a place of powerlessness or fear, for you now understand that you can create the life you desire, or uncreate it simply by lowering or raising the standard or entry point at which others can gain access into your life.

The moment that you realize your worth and value is the moment you set yourself free from anyone or anything that you no longer desire. This is, however, an enormous responsibility to take on and why many choose to stop. They feel they are unwilling to give up some of the "things" they have grown accustomed to having in their lives.

Self-worth

When you arrive at "Self-Worth," there is an indwelling power that allows you to understand you have within you an innate power that can create anything you desire. It is that awareness that allows you to know WHO " I AM." It is an innate knowing who you are, not who others have "told you to be!"

It is about finding your worth, your value deep within your soul self, stepping forward, and being willing to be responsible, even if it doesn't work out quite the way you planned at the moment. The key is that you have the backing of a universal consciousness that will help you find a way to create anything you desire.

Self-worth is about knowing that I am worthy of the things that are now coming into my life.

I have taken the steps one by one, from pain through validation, and now I understand I am worthy of an abundant life. I live in a state of consciousness where I understand that the universe and I are co-creating a life that I wish to live. I understand that I am responsible for the life that I am creating. Therefore, if I do not like something, I am responsible for creating something new.

There is much to be said about being empowered. The moment that you find your power within, everyone around you will notice the difference. Pay close attention to the people who honor you and applaud you coming into your own sense of self. Those are the people who love and support you for being yourself. Some people will tell you that you have changed, and the truth of the matter is that you have. It is the people who relied on you for their wellbeing that will give you the largest pushback. When you found your power, they lost some of theirs. Many may challenge your new-found power and question where your power comes from; however, we know the answer. Realize that anything different, new, strange, out of the normal in our society will cause alarm. People don't like people who stand out. I have found it best never to try to change anyone's mind or to explain my worth/value to anyone. After all, anyone who would question it does not need to be in my life. I bless them and move forward. "What other people think of you is none of your business." If you start to make it your business, you will be offended for the rest of your life. (Deepak Chopra)

Now that I know that, I am a creative being in the universe, just like a drop of the ocean is still the ocean no matter where you take it. We are part of the universe no matter where we go. We have the same creative energy that the universe has, within us at any moment. All we have to do is tap into the universal law that is there for us to use. Just like the bean we planted when we were children. Being a creative being in the universe, realizing our power, we begin to take dominion over our lives. It is at this moment that we start to realize that we are here to evolve and grow. When something or someone comes into our lives, it is not there to punish. It is there to help us grow, and to move forward in love. We create the life we wish to have rather than what we are currently experiencing.

Why would we allow a temporary situation to become a permanent mindset? I do not need to get lost or feel as if I have lost my power. The fact of the matter is the exact opposite. It is a clear manifestation that I am now in a place where I am ready to grow and evolve. To waste my time questioning why this is here and who did this would drain previous energy. I will not lose one moment of my life energy. I shall transform it with love into what I want. I have no business trying to figure out "how, why, when, or where," my work is to set my intention, move upward, and get going. I have the power of the universe at my back, so why would I waste my time or creative energy fighting with something I do not want in my life when I could be creating something I do?

Example:

Intention (a thing intended; an aim, purpose, or plan.)

My intent:

I am open to a healthy, loving and intimate relationship.

At this moment I am showing up in the world as a *"healthy, loving and intimate relationship"*. I no longer need to sit on the sidelines crying about who created this in my life and why this is happening to me. Each of us has to take the time to feel our emotions, and as we express them to the fullest, we allow them a voice. My point here is that we do not make our emotions our permanent dwelling place. You are now a creative being of change who has the power to change anything you like. You have now found your power "within."

Here is where I tell people, "Sunshine shines out of your butt!"

You have had an awakening in life and, come what may, you know you can handle it. You understand that everything in life has a connection to everything; no one is separate from anyone else. You realize that everyone has a path, and regardless of that path, we all find our way home, and love leads the way. No one on this path is lost, and everyone will get there exactly when they are ready. There is no need to push or pull. The only person affected is me, because they are precisely where they need to be at this moment in time. I have found the place within myself where I can love who you are and who I am and know that all is well.

Herein lies the challenge. You may find that many will come seeking your light. Few people are willing to take the steps for themselves. Most people want a shortcut and think they found it in you. It is easy to be tempted to think we can "help/save" others, and I will take this moment to remind you that no one can walk the path for anyone else. Everyone must take their own journey. You may talk about your journey and invite them to take the steps. However, they must find their own way. Be mindful of whom you "give the keys" to your new life.

**People grow when they are ready, not when we "want" them too.*

**No one can force anyone to take this journey.*

**No matter how much "we think" they need*

Step 5

As we set out on this journey, we talked about finding the steps to create a life of freedom in which we would no longer hurt and live lives filled with pain and hurt. The joy of embracing each step along this journey is that we have changed our lives in such a way that many of us may not even recognize the old lives that we left behind. The point of any journey is evolution and growth. We often make it about a destination, yet nothing would have happened without that first step. The Buddha said that "every journey begins with the first step."

Within this book, my intention was to lay out 5 steps that if you EMBRACE them, you will arrive at this final step filled with an empowered love for life, and you will see someone in the mirror each day not only that you like but that you genuinely love. My intention in this step is to have you the reader, understand the essence of who you are and have a love for the self within, unlike anything you have had before. Throughout this journey, the practice of uncovering hidden beliefs and learning there is no need for them to continue to run our lives is due to the fact you are divine and have the power to create the life that you desire.

There is within each of us a connection to every living thing, and at any given moment we can connect to it. Part of that secret is to stop long enough, close our eyes, and allow the silence to reveal itself to us. Once we slow down, we can allow our heart to find its natural rhythm rather than the rhythm that the world has us believe on social media.

Once we remember who we are, we learn to trust our inner wisdom again and, allow it to guide us, rather than having life navigate our emotions. I find that a great deal of us allow what is going on outside to govern how we feel on the inside rather than how we feel on the inside govern our lives on the outside. We understand we now have a power so great, we never have to do that again.

Self-Love/Empowerment

It is the self-realization that you have "self-love." You realize that everyone is part of the same whole that you are. You know that there is only one ocean and that every drop, different as it may be, comes from the same ocean. We are all part of the same universe, learning the same lessons, and there is no need to be sad, mad, or push/pull against anything. Everything in the universe is working for your good. There is an opening within you that allows you to see you are creating everything so that you can evolve and grow and that each lesson in your life is bringing you closer to your true self of pure love.

You realize that you could take offense at what someone says or does, but you would be taking offense at yourself. The person, place, or thing is merely a mirror for growth and evolution. What is being pictured back to you is a reflection of yourself. At that moment, you recognize it and choose to heal the pattern that is being revealed rather than trying to remove it from your existence. At this step, you begin to understand that what you see is yourself at every turn. You can love it, hate it, or heal it. Whatever "it" is, it is you.

The one thing we do to create change on a personal level is to know our actions will affect us and those around us.

Every action we make will impact the world around us. We now live from this place daily. As we do this, we allow others to do the same. We recognize the hurt we see in others as the pain we felt each step of our journey. We realize until they are willing to change that, their lives will remain the same. We see their pain, and we remember how our lives were when we lived in that constant state of pain. We can give them the grace we were unable to provide ourselves with when they say and do things to us that we know they do not mean. We now realize from living a new life free of pain that pain can make us say and do things that we will regret later, and we allow love to show us the way to the life we wish to live on a daily basis.

It is the place within yourself where you empower who you are in the world. You recognize the place in yourself where you know that the Divine and you are one and working together to create a world that is a safe space of all. You recognize that what affects you affects everyone, and what effects everyone affects you. We are the same. We can no longer harm each other without hurting ourselves. We become aware that the need for suffering is useless and that the only purpose in the world is love. You understand that war and pain will continue because many do not understand at this level and that many people choose to live their lives free from the responsibility of anyone other than themselves.

You recognize that Self-love is the greatest gift. When we wholeheartedly love ourselves, we find the secret to loving others where they are. Everyone must take their path and find their way for it to work. Love is the only gift that can be given and never diminished. Few of us understand the meaning of what "giving love" means unless we have taken this journey for ourselves and learned how to love ourselves.

You understand that to give love means to receive it without the attachment of how someone returns it or if they do so at all. You understand that each person on these steps must follow their twists and turns toward self-love. From time to time, your paths will intersect, and you may find that you must take another path than theirs. You remember: No one is lost, and no one is in disrepair. We are all finding our way home.

If we forget ourselves, we merely return to the steps and find our way home again.

When we elevate our lives, our lives change.

As with everything, love changes, evolves, and grows over time. As I mentioned earlier in this step, you can never diminish love, no matter how much you share it with others. What then do we do when we must dismantle love and move in a new direction? For the longest time, I thought that we were to continue loving in the same way, changing nothing, living the way I had as if nothing had changed. I will love you, and you will love me, no matter the time and distance, and we would be one big happy family - until it isn't.

You'll have thirteen cats, and even though the thought of having a cat to me is utterly appalling, life will be excellent. You live on one continent, and I live on another. Or maybe you live on one coast, and I live on the other. (These are only examples.) Many times, we go to great lengths to keep what we call the family together even though we know it has long since been a family.

We will say we are doing this for the children when, in fact, we are unwilling to let go of the relationship ourselves. Saying goodbye doesn't mean that it is the end; it merely means we are willing to allow everyone the freedom to find what they need, ourselves included. It is also the opening for a greater yet to be. Far too often, we hold on too long, which closes off any hope of anything in the future. We have lost our trust in the universe and the fact that we are part of everything and everyone.

How do I let go in love?

Love will always want you to:

Grow!
Evolve!
Leave the nest.
Believe in yourself.
Know that you are supported and loved.
Never look back; the answer is not back there.
Follow your heart/your inner wisdom.

Most often we get stuck trying to hold on to what we have and grab what we want at the same time. We can't have both! If your arms are full holding what you have, you have no room for what you want. You have to choose. You will need to decide which one you want before you can move forward. You need to go back a step and clear and clean your way for a new crop. Then move forward again.

Please understand me: I am not speaking about affection.

I am talking about when a life situation changes our life or the lives of those we love. You find yourselves in love with each other, yet life has rearranged the placement, and you understand that one or both of you may need to leave the nest so that you live at your fullest potential

Laurie F. has been such a gift in my life. In step 2, she and I create a friendship that started with an interview that would forever change my life. Not only did it change it, it changed the way I looked at relationships going forward. That year, our relationship as friends had some significant twists and turns. We were, however, able to handle everything that came our way, due to what we laid out in the beginning.

When we found ourselves at the end of what had been a vibrant part of our lives, we knew that it was going to impact our lives and the lives of the community around us. We had created a sacred tribe of friends that would be affected by this change as well. As much as any of us would like to "make believe" it would go on like this forever, the truth is many of us would never see each other again. When life happens, we have no intent to grow in new directions; however, it does happen.

The big leap!

We meet new people, we fall in love, and we move on. Laurie and I created this incredible friendship, and we wanted to honor what we created to remember the greatness of that moment. We understood we would never be the same, and we needed to acknowledge that moment in time. I would soon be moving away from her, and as much as we would miss our friendship, we knew it was time for me to spread my wings and fly.

We needed to have closure so that we could create an opening for what was next. It felt like we were at the beginning all over again, except this time I knew it would be different. We wouldn't see each other every day, and we wouldn't talk to each other all the time. Laurie asked me for a three-month break to heal, unless I needed something, or I was hurt. It worked out well, as I was on a singing tour, and needed some time not to miss her, or to change my mind and come back home. I was beginning to understand what love feels like when it leaves the nest and sends you off.

It doesn't diminish.
It wants only the best for you.
Love only wishes you joy, safety, and happiness.

What were our expectations?
*We were never going to be as close as we once had been.
*We would always love each other and wanted the best for both.
*Regardless of time and distance if we needed anything reach out.
*We both still loved each other.

Love pushes those we love out of the nest to their own highest adventure, even when we understand that it will cause us pain, growth, and evolution. How do we create the close of one relationship and the opening for a new one at the same time?

We look at where we started and remember the tools we picked up along the way. We love the person, and while we want to keep them in our lives, we realize that we also want them to have the experience they deserve. We, therefore, need to create a celebration that honors all of who we have been together with the intent to bless them on their way as they take flight to their new life with our blessing.

Have a nice dinner with your best china (if you enjoy that).

Have a kid's party (if you enjoy that).

Book a women day at the spa.

Have a man's night out at the pub.

Whatever it is, make sure everyone understands that it is a celebration that honors all of who you were. Bring everything to the table: every tear, laugh, pictures, jokes, fun, dancing; this is the last moment you will be together in (this form) as a group. Celebrate it! Enjoy it! You may meet again in five months or a year, but trust me when I say everything will change. Change is the one constant we can depend on in life.

I Can Handle A New Growth Experience!

If possible, at the end of the evening, I suggest you come together and light a candle, take a picture, sing a song - something special that ends that night and honors the person who is moving. It is the realization that this group will no longer be the same group again.

You now have a choice.

Feel your emotions and know that love will show you the way.

Create a new group without this person.

Never meet again.

Act as if nothing happened.

When we create closure in a relationship, it allows us to move forward freely.

The beauty of what happened above means that I can still be in a relationship with everyone, and I can move forward as well. I realize I am growing, and if I think my friends are going to remain the same while I am out seeing the world, what sense would that make? They are out flying as well. Our relationship has changed, and we need to adjust to that fact. We are different, and more than likely, so are they.

As we grow and evolve, we are bound to cross paths, meet along the way, walk the same path again. As we journey together, we are wiser and stronger. We know the steps to take to ensure a loving and healthy relationship.

Final Words

My intent with this book was for you, the reader, to find a step that you could identify with, then plant your seed and begin to grow. Every person in the universe is expanding; otherwise, we are dead. We are part of an ever-growing, multi-diverse universe that expands every day. If we think for a moment that we are exempt from that, we are sadly mistaken. The whole point of evolution was to be part of this wondrous experience and have a chance to grow and evolve. Many of us have forgotten that agreement and lost sight of who we are and why we came here in the first place. Our mission in life is to rediscover that at any cost.

The universe will help us do that one way or another. We can do that with our eyes wide open or with blinders on, chasing what everyone else is chasing, thinking it will bring us happiness, love, fulfillment, and joy, only to get there, in the end, to find that it is empty and wonder, "Where do we go from here?" Holding a safe space for others means allowing them to find their way when they are ready, not when I am ready. It means allowing others to take the path they need rather than the path I want them to take, and the path I know would be the best for them as they journey along. I never listened to anyone as they did their best to guide me, and I found my way in the end, and I know the same is true for everyone else as well. Today, I know that no one is lost, and no one is broken. We are all just walking each other home. Can I find within myself enough love, kindness, and compassion to allow them the grace that someone gave me as I was finding my way home? That is my plan, purpose, and commitment.

I no longer need to be a doormat while they do that. I no longer need to give anyone the answers or diminish myself in the process. I will love them and honor them; however, I no longer need to be around them as they figure this out for themselves. My responsibility ends with myself. As I stand in their goodness, it no longer requires me to hold them up, or go in the cave after them, or as my friend Ron says, "breathe for them." For the longest time, I thought I had to save the world, and today I know that the only person I have to save is myself. The greatest gift my husband and I gave each other was that awareness. As much as we love each other and care for each other, we are fully aware that we are only responsible for ourselves. Out of that responsibility has come this precious and abiding love like I have never had before. When I am fully responsible for myself, I can love and care for another person by choice and give a gift of love. As we spoke of in the last step, love is constant. It is something that doesn't diminish and go away. Once I know that I have taken responsibility for my life, I now know that I have the willingness not only to love myself; I cannot give that love to someone with abandon, without condition, and as I do so, I know what it means when I say for better or worse.

I had the opportunity to have a conversation with a friend the other day. My friend is someone who has used the five-step method in their life, and it changed their life dramatically. They were thanking me for sharing the information and saying how much it had impacted their lives. We spoke about how we all need boundaries and that as we build them, we can raise and lower them every day, and as we do that, we will find that our pain level will go up and down as a result of it. Their question was, "How long do we have to do this?" My response was, "Every day that we don't want to hurt." Most often, we forget that we enter into new relationships every day, and as we do that, we need to set new boundaries, have interviews, and create guidelines for ourselves and those we love.

Life is a beautiful garden; fill it with love, water it daily, tend the boundaries, weed when necessary, and enjoy the harvest.

You are deeply loved.